Discovering Religions

Judaism

FOUNDATION EDITION

SUE PENNEY

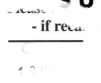

Heinemann Educational Publishers
Halley Court, Jordan Hill, Oxford OX2 8EJ
a division of Reed Educational & Professional Publishing Ltd

OXFORD MELBOURNE AUCKLAND
JOHANNESBURG BLANTYRE GABORONE
IBADAN PORTSMOUTH NH (US) CHICAGO

Heinemann is a registered trademark of Reed Educational & Professional Publishing
Ltd

03 02 01
10 9 8 7 6 5 4

British Library Cataloguing in Publication Data

ISBN 0 435 30474 7

Designed and typeset by Visual Image
Illustrated by Gecko Limited. Adapted into colour by Visual Image
Cover design by Keith Shaw at Threefold Design
Printed and bound in Great Britain by Bath Colourbooks, Glasgow

Acknowledgements

The publishers would like to thank the following for permission to use photographs:
The Ancient Art and Architecture Collection p. 39; Werner Braun pp. 40 (top), 42
(top), 44; J Allan Cash Photo Library p. 32; Circa Photo Library pp. 12, 17; Bruce
Coleman Ltd p. 25; A H Edwards/Circa Photo Library p. 13; Robert Harding pp. 6, 38;
The Hutchinson Library p. 16; Jewish Education Bureau p. 8; The Jewish Museum p.
23; B Key/Christine Osborne Pictures p. 37; Peter Osborne p. 40 (below); Zev
Radovan pp. 33, 34; Anat Rotem-Braun p. 21; Barrie Searle/Circa Photo Library pp.
11, 27, 29, 31; Juliette Soester pp. 10, 14, 18 (below), 28, 42 (below), 45, 47; The
Weiner Library p. 36; Zefa pp. 7, 9, 15, 18 (top), 20, 22, 26, 46.

The publishers would like to thank Zefa for permission to reproduce the cover
photograph.

The publishers have made every effort to trace copyright holders. However, if any
material has been incorrectly acknowledged we would be pleased to correct this at
the earliest opportunity.

Contents

MAP: where the main religions began

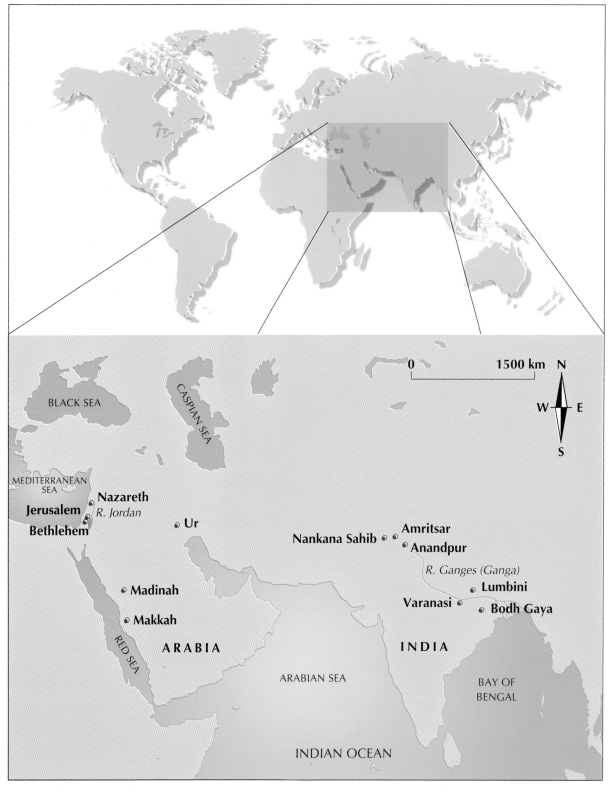

BLACK SEA

CASPIAN SEA

MEDITERRANEAN
SEA

Nazareth
Jerusalem
R. Jordan
Bethlehem

Ur

Nankana Sahib

Amritsar
Anandpur

R. Ganges (Ganga)

Lumbini

Madinah

Varanasi

Bodh Gaya

Makkah

RED SEA

ARABIA

INDIA

ARABIAN SEA

BAY OF
BENGAL

0   1500 km   N

W   E

S

INDIAN OCEAN

TIMECHART: when the main religions began

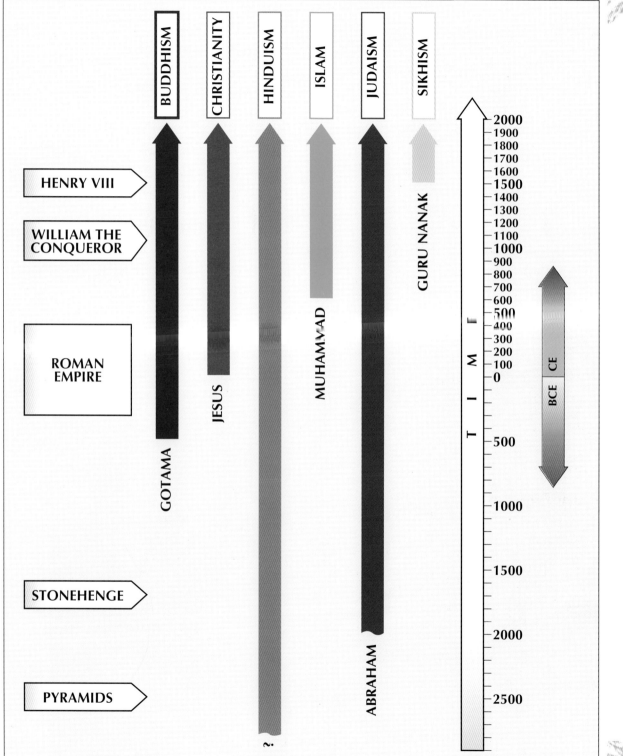

Note about dating systems In this book dates are not called BC and AD which is the Christian dating system. The letters BCE and CE are used instead. BCE stands for 'Before the Common Era' and CE stands for 'Common Era'. BCE and CE can be used by people of all religions, Christians too. The year numbers are not changed.

Introducing Judaism

This section tells you something about what Jews believe.

What is Judaism?

Judaism is the religion of people who are Jews. Judaism is one of the oldest religions in the world.

What do Jews believe?

Jews believe that there is one God. Although they call God 'he', they do not believe that God is really male. They believe he is a spirit, without a body. They believe he is **eternal**, so was never born and will never die. He is everywhere and knows everything. He made everything and cares about what he made. He listens when people pray to him.

The names of God

Jews have several names for God, but they use one name more than others. They call him **Adonai**. Adonai means Lord. Jews believe that God's name is very important. They never use it carelessly.

God's relationship with the Jews

Jews believe they have a special relationship with God. They believe God gave them

A modern sculpture of a menorah

The Star of David

important place of worship for the Jews. It was destroyed by the Romans in 70 CE.

Another symbol which is often used is a star with six points. No one really knows where this symbol came from, but it has been used for hundreds of years. It is called the Star of David.

laws which they must obey. If they obey the laws, God will look after them. Jews believe that the most important law is to love God. The prayer called the **Shema** shows this. It says 'You must love the Lord your God with all your heart, with all your mind and with all your strength'.

Symbols which Jews use

Jews often use the **symbol** of a candlestick with seven branches. It is called a **menorah**. It reminds Jews of the lamp which used to burn in the **Temple** in Jerusalem. The Temple was the most

New words

Adonai 'Lord' – Jewish name for God
Eternal lasting for ever
Menorah candlestick with seven branches
Shema most important Jewish prayer
Symbol something that stands for something else
Temple most important place of worship for Jews

Test yourself

What does Adonai mean?

What is the Shema?

What is a menorah?

What was the Temple?

Describe the Star of David.

Think it through

1 Use the information here to explain as carefully as you can what Jews believe about God.

2 What do you think it means to love someone with all your heart, mind and strength?

3 Jews use God's name with great respect. Think of something or someone in your life that you respect. How do you show what you feel?

The synagogue

This section tells you about the place where Jews meet to worship God.

Jews go to a **synagogue** to worship God. The main room is used for worship, but there are usually other rooms, too. Jewish children have classes in the synagogue where they learn about Judaism. They also learn **Hebrew** there. This is the language the Jewish **holy** books are written in.

The Ark

The most important thing in the synagogue is the **Ark**. This is a special cupboard. It is always at the front of the main room. The **scrolls** are kept in it.

Scrolls

A scroll is like a book with one long page. It is made from **parchment**. This is animal skin which has been dried and smoothed so that it can be written on. The scroll is wound around wooden rollers. You unroll the page to read it. If the page is unwound fully, it is about 60 metres long. The writing on the scrolls is done by hand, using special ink. The scrolls are precious because the **Torah** is written on them. Another name for the Torah is the Books of Teaching. Jews believe the Torah contains the teaching which God gave, which Jews must follow.

When a scroll is going to be read in a synagogue service, it is taken out of the Ark. It is carried carefully through the synagogue to the **bimah**. This is a raised part of the floor in the middle of the synagogue. It has a reading desk on it. The scroll is put here

Inside a modern synagogue. The seats upstairs are the women's section

to be read. Before it is put away in the Ark, the scroll is wrapped in a beautiful cover.

The lamp

In front of the Ark is a special lamp. It burns all the time. It reminds Jews that God is

The Ark is at the front of the synagogue

always with them. It also reminds Jews of the lamp which used to burn in the Temple.

The women's section

In most synagogues, men and women do not sit together. Women have a separate part of their own.

Test yourself

What is a synagogue?

Where is the Ark?

What is a scroll made of?

What is the Torah?

Where is the bimah?

Think it through

1 Use the information and the pictures on this page, and the pictures on page 12–13, to help you write a short description of the Ark and the scrolls.

2 How many reasons can you think of why Jews use the synagogue as a place to teach children?

3 If it is possible, arrange to go and visit a synagogue. If you cannot, use books and videos to find out as much as you can about them. Make a model, or do a project with a description and pictures.

New words

Ark cupboard where the scrolls are kept

Bimah raised part of the floor where the reading desk is

Hebrew language of the Jews

Holy to do with God

Parchment writing surface made from animal skin

Scrolls rolled up 'books' on which the Torah is written

Synagogue Jewish place of worship

Torah Books of Teaching (part of the Jewish holy books)

Worship in the synagogue

This section tells you about how Jews worship in the synagogue.

A synagogue service

Many Jews go to the synagogue on a Friday evening or a Saturday. This is the Jewish holy day. As they go into the synagogue, Jews wash their hands. This is a way of saying they want to be fit to worship God. Then they say a prayer which thanks God that they can worship him.

A synagogue service has readings from the holy books, prayers and **psalms**. A psalm is a special poem. Some services also include readings from the Torah. The Torah scroll is carried from the Ark to the bimah, and carefully unwrapped. After the reading is finished, it is carried back again.

A full synagogue service can only be held if there are more than ten men present. If there are not, some of the prayers are not said.

This boy is dressed for worship

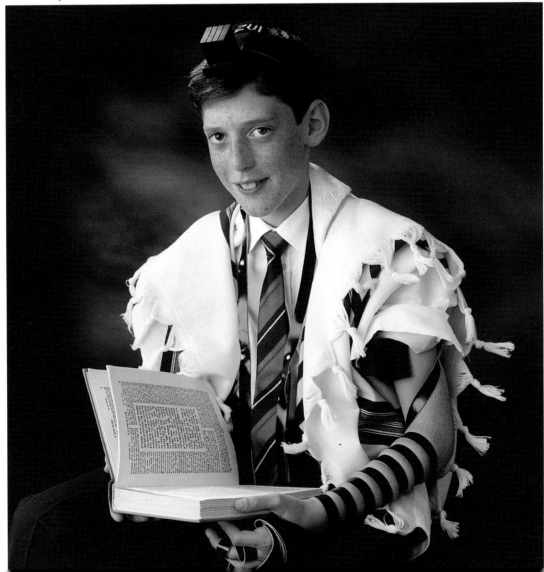

Clothes for worship

For services in the synagogue, men wear a **kippah**. This is a skull cap. It often has beautiful embroidery on it. Wearing a kippah is a sign of respect for God. At morning services, men wear a **tallit**, too. This is a special prayer robe which is worn like a large scarf. It is usually made of silk or wool. It has tassels at each end.

In some synagogues, men also wear two small black leather boxes. They have long straps and are tied to the arm and the head. The boxes are called **tefillin** (one is called a tefillah). They contain small pieces of parchment. They have verses from the Torah written on them. The box that is worn on the forehead reminds Jews to love God with all their mind. The one worn on the arm faces the heart, so it reminds Jews to love God with all their heart.

A tefillah and its contents

New words

Kippah skull cap
Psalms sorts of poem used in worship
Tallit prayer robe
Tefillin small leather boxes which contain writings from the Torah (one is called a tefillah)

Test yourself

When is the Jewish holy day?

What is a kippah?

What is a tallit?

What are tefillin?

Where are tefillin worn?

Think it through

1 Describe the special clothes which a Jewish man wears for worship. When does he wear them?

2 Why do you think ten men have to be present before a full synagogue service can be held?

3 Many synagogues are beautifully decorated, and so are some of the things used there. What does this tell you about how Jews feel about their worship? What sort of things do you look after carefully? Why?

Jewish holy books

This section tells you about the Jewish holy books.

The Jewish holy books are called the **Tenakh**. They are divided into three parts. The first part is called the Torah. The second part is called Nevi'im. The third part is called Ketuvim. The word Tenakh comes from the first letters of these three names.

The Torah

Torah means the Books of Teaching. The books of the Torah are the most important books for Jews. They are the ones that are written on scrolls for reading in the synagogue. They begin with stories about how the world was made and about the very first Jews.

They are called the Books of Teaching because they include the rules which teach Jews how they should live. Altogether there are 613 rules in the Torah. They are about many different parts of life. Some Jews follow these rules very strictly because they believe it means they are living in the way God wants.

Nevi'im

Nevi'im means the Books of the **Prophets**. A prophet is someone who is a messenger from God. Jews believe that God gave the

Scrolls with their covers and decorations

A scroll on the bimah. Notice the pointer which is used when the scroll is being read

prophets special power. This meant that they could tell people how God wanted them to live. Jews believe that what the prophets said is still important for people today. Some of the books are read in services in the synagogue. They are usually read from an ordinary book, not a scroll. Other parts of Nevi'im may be read by Jews at home.

Ketuvim

Ketuvim are the Books of **Writings**. These books contain stories from Jewish history. The best known of these books is the Book of Psalms. A psalm is a special sort of poem. Psalms are often used in services in the synagogue.

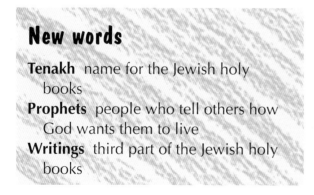

New words

Tenakh name for the Jewish holy books
Prophets people who tell others how God wants them to live
Writings third part of the Jewish holy books

Test yourself

What is the Tenakh?

What is the Torah?

Why are the books of the Torah so important?

What is a prophet?

What is a psalm?

Think it through

1 What are the names of the three parts of the Jewish holy books? Copy the shapes below and fit them together to show how the complete holy books make the Tenakh.

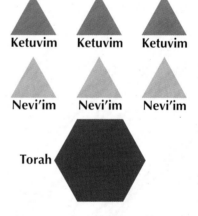

The Tenakh

2 Why do Jews follow the rules of the Torah? Explain why some Jews might follow them more strictly than others.

3 The prophets believed that God was giving them messages for the people about how they should live. What sort of messages might someone living in Britain today give people?

Shabbat

This section tells you about the Jewish day of worship.

Shabbat is the Jewish day for rest and worship. It begins when the sun sets on a Friday evening. It lasts until sunset on Saturday. All Jewish days begin at sunset.

Why do Jews celebrate Shabbat?

The Jewish holy books say that God made the world in six days. On the seventh day he rested. To remember this, Jews rest on the seventh day of the week, too.

How do Jews celebrate Shabbat?

On Fridays, Jews clean the house and get ready for the special Shabbat meal. At sunset, the wife or mother of the family begins the Shabbat celebrations. She lights two candles and says a special prayer. Shabbat has begun!

After this, many families go to the synagogue. When they come home, the father says prayers. He asks God to look after the children in the family and he reads from the holy books. Then everyone eats the meal together. As it begins, the father says a special prayer called the **kiddush**. This praises God, and thanks him that Jews can share in Shabbat.

The Shabbat meal is the most important meal of the week. The table is always set with a clean white cloth and the food is the best the family can afford. The meal always includes two loaves of special bread. This is called **challah bread**. The meal is a happy, relaxed occasion. Many families spend all evening eating and chatting.

The day of rest

The Torah tells Jews that they should rest on Shabbat. Many Jews follow this rule very carefully. Resting means more than just not

Lighting the Shabbat candles. Notice the challah bread under its cover

working. They do not drive or go shopping. Cooking is not allowed, so all food is prepared the day before. Some Jews will not switch on a light or use a telephone, except in an emergency.

Keeping Shabbat like this makes it a day which is different from all other days. Jews can spend the day with friends or family without feeling that they should be doing something.

Shabbat ends on a Saturday evening with another prayer, called the **havdalah**. Jews light a special plaited candle. Everyone sniffs a spice box, too. The sweet smell of the spices spreads all through the house. It is a way of showing that they hope the peace and quiet of Shabbat will last all through the coming week. Shabbat is over when three stars can be seen in the sky.

The havdalah ceremony. Notice the candle and the spice box

New words

Challah bread special bread for Shabbat

Kiddush prayer which begins the Shabbat meal

Havdalah prayer said at the end of Shabbat

Test yourself

When is Shabbat?

Why do Jews celebrate Shabbat?

What is challah bread?

What is kiddush?

What are the prayers that end Shabbat called?

Think it through

1 Shabbat is sometimes called 'Queen Shabbat'. Why do you think it is given this name?

2 The wife or mother always begins the Shabbat celebrations. One of the passages from the holy books which the father reads praises women. Why do you think women are so important in the celebrations? Give reasons for your answer.

3 Jews look forward to Shabbat every week. Why do you think they enjoy it so much?

Rosh Hashanah and Yom Kippur

This section tells you what happens around the time of Jewish New Year.

Rosh Hashanah

Rosh Hashanah is the Jewish New Year. Jews have their own calendar, and New Year is in late September or early October. Jewish years have their own numbers, too. They are 3761 years ahead of the calendar used in most Western countries.

A special meal

On the evening before Rosh Hashanah, Jews eat a special meal at home. As part of the meal, they eat apples dipped in honey. This is a way of saying that they hope the year that is coming will be sweet – in other words, a good one.

Jews eat apples and honey at Rosh Hashanah

A special service

At Rosh Hashanah there is a special service in the synagogue. The **shofar** is blown. This is a musical instrument made from a ram's horn. It sounds a bit like a trumpet. It is very loud and solemn. At Rosh Hashanah, the shofar is blown 100 times. It reminds Jews that God is very powerful.

The Days of Returning

Rosh Hashanah is the first of ten special days for Jews called the Days of Returning. It is a time when Jews think about the things they did wrong in the past year. They promise themselves and God to do better next year. The last of the days is Yom Kippur.

Yom Kippur

Yom Kippur means the Day of **Atonement**. It is the most solemn day of the year. Atonement means making up for something

Blowing the shofar at the end of Yom Kippur

you have done wrong. Jews pray to God to forgive them for the wrong things they have done. They **fast** for 25 hours and spend a lot of the day at the synagogue.

Jews believe that, if they are really sorry, God will forgive them because he loves them. So Yom Kippur also remembers how kind God is. The Ark and the reading desk are covered in white cloths. The people leading the service wear white, too. White is a symbol. It shows that God will take away sins and leave the people 'clean'.

At the end of the service, the shofar is blown again. It reminds Jews of the promises they have made. It reminds them to try and live good lives in the coming year.

New words

Atonement making up for something you have done wrong

Fast go without food and drink for religious reasons

Shofar instrument made from a ram's horn

Test yourself

What is Jewish New Year called?

What does Yom Kippur mean?

What does atonement mean?

What is a shofar?

What is fasting?

Think it through

1 Look at the picture on this page. Explain what the man is doing, and why he is doing it. What is he wearing? Why?

2 The days between Rosh Hashanah and Yom Kippur are called the Days of Returning. Why do you think they have this name?

3 Why do you think Jews fast to show that they are sorry? What sort of things do you do to show that you are sorry about something?

Sukkot

This section tells you about the festival of Sukkot.

A **sukkah** is a sort of hut. Sukkot is the word for more than one sukkah. For the festival of Sukkot, Jews build a sukkah in their garden or at the synagogue. They live in it for the week of the festival.

A sukkah is usually made of wood. The roof is made of branches. It must be open enough for you to see the sky. Jews often hang fruit from the roof.

A sukkah

Why do Jews build sukkot?

Thousands of years ago, Jews had no fixed home. They spent many years in the desert.

Some Jews probably had tents. Others had to build themselves somewhere to live. They built sukkot. Today, Jews build sukkot to remind themselves of the time when Jewish people had nowhere else to live.

Holding the lulav and the citron

In the synagogue

There is a special service in the synagogue at Sukkot. Everyone holds branches of three trees in their right hand, and a citron in their left hand. A citron is a yellow fruit rather like a lemon. During the synagogue service, everyone walks round the synagogue carrying these things. The branches are waved in all directions to show that God rules all the universe.

The branches are called the **lulav**. They come from the palm, willow and myrtle trees. They are tied together, and are symbols. The palm tree stands for the spine. The willow stands for the lips. The myrtle stands for the eyes. The citron stands for the heart. Together, these things remind Jews that they must worship God with their whole body.

Simchat Torah

The day after the end of Sukkot is called Simchat Torah. It is a day when Jews think especially about the Torah. Part of the Torah is read in the services in the synagogue every week, so that it is read all the way through during the year. Simchat Torah is the day when the last part of the Torah is read and the readings start again from the beginning. It is a very happy day. The scrolls are taken out of the Ark and carried around the synagogue, with people dancing, singing and clapping after them. To celebrate the festival, children in the synagogue are often given bags of sweets and fruit.

New words

Lulav collection of branches for Sukkot
Sukkah sort of hut (plural sukkot)

Test yourself

What is a sukkah?

What do sukkot remind Jews of?

What is the lulav?

What is a citron?

Why are the branches waved in all directions?

Think it through

1 Why do you think Jews hang fruit from the roof of the sukkah? Why must it be open to the sky?

2 Jews believe that the Torah shows the way God wants them to live. Why do you think the readings always go back to the beginning as soon as they reach the end?

3 What do you think it is like to camp in a sukkah? Write a few sentences saying what you think it would be like. Describe what the sukkah looks like, too.

Hanukkah

This section tells you about the festival of Hanukkah.

Hanukkah usually takes place at the beginning of December. It lasts for eight days. Jews celebrate it with parties and presents, and there are special games. Another name for Hanukkah is the festival of Lights.

The story of Hanukkah

At Hanukkah, Jews remember a story from over 2000 years ago. The Jews' country had been taken over by a wicked king called Antiochus. He would not allow the Jews to worship God. He said they had to worship him! The Jews knew that he was only a man and that it would be wrong to worship him.

A group of Jews fought against the king. They were led by a man called Judah. After three years of fighting, Judah and his men managed to capture Jerusalem. This was important because the Temple was there. The Temple was the most important place for worshipping God. Antiochus had tried to spoil the Temple, so that the Jews could not use it.

Judah wanted to make the Temple fit to worship God again. It had to be carefully cleaned. Then the menorah could be lit. This was the Temple lamp, which had seven branches. It was supposed to burn all the time, but Antiochus had let it go out. When Judah's soldiers came to light the lamp again, they found that there was only enough oil for one night. The oil was special, and it took eight days to get more. But the lamp stayed alight all the time. The people said that this was a **miracle**. God had made it burn because he was so pleased to be worshipped in the Temple again.

Lighting the candles at Hanukkah

Celebrating Hanukkah

Jews use a special candlestick when they are celebrating Hanukkah. It is called a **hanukiah**. It holds eight candles, and an extra one called the 'servant candle' which is used to light all the others. On the first

Playing the dreidle game

New words

Dreidle four-sided spinning top
Hanukiah candlestick with eight
   branches used at Hanukkah
Miracle event which can't be explained
   but which shows God's power

Test Yourself

Who was Antiochus?

Who was Judah?

What is a miracle?

What is a hanukiah?

What is a dreidle?

night of the festival, one candle is lit, two
are lit on the second night and so on. On
the last night, all nine are lit. As Jews light
the candles, they say special prayers.

The dreidle game

Hanukkah is a very happy time. Children go
to parties and give each other presents.
Many Jewish children play with a special
spinning top. It is called a **dreidle**. It has
four sides. On each side there is a letter
from the Hebrew alphabet. When the
letters are put together, they make the first
letters of the words which say 'A great
miracle happened here'. Children play the
game with sweets. They spin the dreidle
and the letter it lands on tells them whether
to take all the sweets, take none, give back
what they have or do nothing.

Think it through

1 Judah's nickname was Maccabee.
This means 'the hammer'. What
does this tell you about the sort of
man he was? What do you think the
other Jews thought about him?

2 Look carefully at the hanukiah in the
pictures. Describe what they are like
and how they are used.

3 How do you think the Jews felt about
not being able to use their Temple?
How would you feel if something
that was important to you had been
spoiled by someone who was bigger
or stronger? How would you feel if
someone else made it right again?

Purim

This section tells you about the festival of Purim.

Purim is the story of a good queen and a bad man. It is a very exciting festival. The story is in the Jewish holy books and in the Bible. It is called the Book of Esther.

The story of Purim

Hundreds of years ago, a man called Haman lived in a country called Persia. Haman helped the king to rule the country, and he liked being important. He expected everyone to bow as he passed. Some Jews lived in Persia then. Jews believe that bowing to someone means worshipping them, and that it is wrong to worship anyone but God. So they would not bow to Haman.

Haman did not like the Jews. One day when a Jew did not bow as he passed, Haman became very angry. He decided to get rid of all the Jews in Persia. He went to the king and told lies about the Jews, saying they were dangerous. The king agreed that all the Jews in the country should be killed.

Queen Esther heard about this. She was Jewish, but the king did not know this. She wanted to save her people, but it was

A play for Purim

This old scroll of the Book of Esther is in the Jewish Museum in London

difficult. She needed to get the king to change his mind. However, she was only supposed to see him when he sent for her! She was very brave. She invited the king and Haman to a special meal. During the meal she told the king the real reason why Haman wanted the Jews killed. The king was very angry. He ordered that Haman should be killed instead. All the Jews were saved.

Celebrating Purim

At Purim, this story is read in the synagogue. Every time children hear Haman's name, they make as much noise as they possibly can. They hiss and stamp their feet. They use whistles and special rattles called **greggors**. The idea is to make so much noise that Haman's name can't be heard at all.

Children often go to fancy dress parties at Purim. They may take part in plays about the story, too.

New word

Greggors rattles used by children at Purim

Test yourself

Where did this story take place?

Who was Esther?

Who was Haman?

Why was Haman angry?

What is a greggor?

Think it through

1 Why did Haman want to get rid of all the Jews? Do you think Haman deserved what happened to him?

2 Jews often give money to poorer people at Purim. What reasons can you think of why they do this?

3 Working in groups, make up a play or a mime to tell the story of Purim.

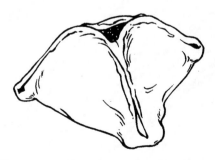

A Hamantaschen, eaten at Purim

Pesach

This section tells you about the story of Pesach.

Pesach is the most important Jewish festival. It remembers events which happened nearly 4000 years ago. It is also called the festival of Passover.

The story of Passover

Jews were living in the country called Egypt. The king of Egypt made them work for him. They were slaves, so they were not paid. They were beaten if they did not work hard enough.

One of the Jews was called Moses. He believed that God was telling him to rescue his people. Moses went to the king and told him that he must free the Jews. The king did not like the Jews, but he did like the work they were doing. He refused to let them go.

The ten plagues

After this, dreadful things started to happen. They were called **plagues**. Everyone believed the plagues were sent by God. Each time there was a plague, the king said that the Jews could go. But as soon as it stopped, he changed his mind again.

The ten plagues

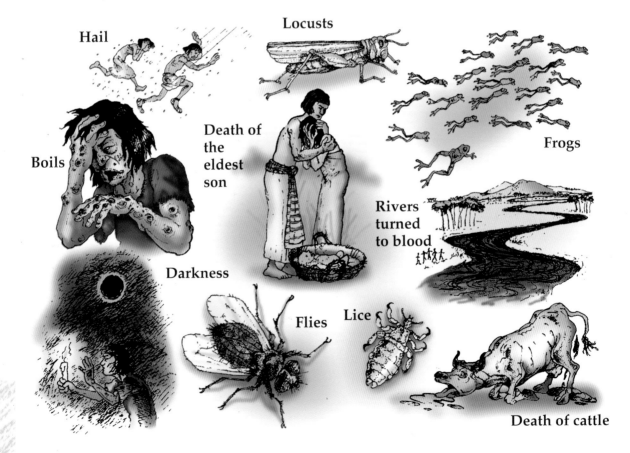

Hail

Locusts

Boils

Death of the eldest son

Frogs

Rivers turned to blood

Darkness

Flies

Lice

Death of cattle

The tenth plague was the worst of all. The eldest son in every Egyptian family died, including the king's son. The king was so upset that he said this time the Jews really could go. The Jews escaped as quickly as they could. But even then, the king changed his mind. He sent his army after the Jews as they were escaping. The Jews were saved because the water in the Sea of Reeds parted to allow them to cross. Then it flooded back and the army was drowned.

At Passover, Jews remember how God cared for them. They call it Passover because they remember that death passed over the houses of the Jews, and the Jews passed over the Sea of Reeds.

New words

Plagues disasters believed to be sent by God

Test yourself

What is a slave?

What did Moses say to the king?

What is a plague?

How many plagues were there?

Why is the festival called Passover?

Think it through

1 Look at the picture of the plagues. Choose the three plagues that you think were the worst. Say what you think it must have been like in Egypt when they were happening.

2 What sort of a person do you think the king of Egypt was? Why do you think he kept changing his mind?

3 Working in small groups, discuss what you think it would feel like to be a slave. Write a poem or draw a picture to show your ideas.

Locusts were the eighth plague

Celebrating Pesach

This section tells you about how Jews celebrate Pesach, or Passover.

Before Passover begins, all **leaven** is removed from the house. Leaven is an ingredient like baking powder or yeast which makes dough rise. It is removed to remind Jews that when the people were escaping from Egypt, there was no time to let bread rise. Nothing containing leaven is eaten during the festival.

The Seder

The most important part of the celebration of Pesach is a meal. It is called the **Seder**. During the meal, the youngest person there asks four questions about the foods they are eating and why they are special. The oldest person answers them. The answers tell the story of the first Passover.

The Seder is a normal meal, but it always includes five special foods. They are on a special plate, and remind Jews of what happened in Egypt.

Special foods for the Seder

- A lamb bone. This is not eaten, but it reminds Jews of the lambs killed in Egypt.
- A hard-boiled egg. This is roasted in a flame and reminds Jews of the animals killed as an offering to God.
- A green vegetable. This is usually parsley or lettuce and reminds Jews of the way God cared for them in the desert.
- Bitter herbs. This is usually horseradish and reminds Jews of how unhappy they were in Egypt.
- Charoset. This is a sweet mixture of apples, nuts and wine. It is a paste, so it reminds Jews of the mortar which the slaves used when they were building. It is also sweet, so it reminds them of the happiness of escape.

Three other things are also on the table for the Seder.
- A dish containing **matzot**. Matzot are rather like crackers – flat 'cakes' of unleavened bread.

The Seder meal

The Seder plate with matzot

Test yourself

What is leaven?

Why don't Jews eat leaven during Passover?

What is the Seder?

What are matzot?

What is charoset?

Think it through

1 Choose three of the special foods which are eaten at the Seder. Explain why they are eaten and why they are symbols.

2 Why do you think Jews feel it is a good idea to remind themselves every year of something which happened so long ago?

3 If possible, prepare some or all of a Passover meal as a class. If this is not possible, work in groups to make a wall chart showing the story of Passover and how Jews celebrate it.

- A bowl of salt water. This is not to drink. It is to remind Jews of the tears which they cried, because they were so unhappy in Egypt.
- A wine glass for each person. Wine is drunk four times during the meal, because God promised four times that he would bring the Jews out of Egypt.

A family occasion

The Seder is a serious meal, because it reminds Jews of their history. But it is also a time when families can relax and enjoy being together. When they have finished eating, they often stay at the table singing songs. The songs have repeated words and choruses, so even small children can enjoy joining in. It all helps to make Pesach a special time.

Shavuot

This section tells you about the festival of Shavuot.

The festival of Shavuot is held seven weeks after Pesach. It is sometimes called the Feast of Weeks. At Shavuot, Jews remember a story from the Torah. The story is about how God gave Moses the ten special rules that tell people how they should live. These rules are called the Ten **Commandments**. Jews believe they are very important.

The Ten Commandments

In the Torah, the Ten Commandments are quite long, but the rules they give can be summed up like this.

1 I am the Lord your God. You must not have any other gods but me.
2 You must not make any **idols** to worship.
3 You must not use God's name carelessly.
4 Remember to keep Shabbat holy.
5 Respect your father and your mother.
6 You must not murder.

Synagogues are decorated for Shavuot

7 You must not commit **adultery**.

8 You must not steal.

9 You must not tell lies about other people.

10 You must not be jealous of other people's possessions.

Celebrating Shavuot

At Shavuot, synagogues are always beautifully decorated with flowers and fruit. There is a special service when Jews read the story from the Torah about how Moses went up Mount Sinai to talk to God. When Moses came down, God had given him the Ten Commandments.

After the service In the synagogue, Jews go home for a meal. Like other festival meals, there is always bread which has been specially baked. For Shavuot, the bread has a ladder shape on it. This is to remind people of climbing, because Moses climbed the mountain to talk to God.

Ladder bread

New words

Adultery sexual relationship outside marriage

Commandments important rules

Idols false gods (often statues)

Test yourself

What is another name for Shavuot?

How is the synagogue decorated?

What is a commandment?

Where did Moses talk to God?

Why does Shavuot bread have a ladder on it?

Think it through

1 Why do Jews believe that the Ten Commandments are so important? What is your opinion of them? Is there anything you would like to add or take away?

2 Why do you think bread is often a part of the special festival meals which Jews eat?

3 What is an idol? What sort of idols do you think people might worship today?

Jewish history

This section tells you something about early Jewish history.

Jewish history began about 4000 years ago. No one person ever 'began' Judaism. People had ideas which slowly grew. They became beliefs. The people became sure the beliefs came from God. They began to live in a way which showed what they believed. Beliefs were passed down from parents to children. Over hundreds of years, Jews became different from the people who lived around them. Judaism had begun!

Abraham and Moses

Abraham and Moses were two of the great leaders at the beginning of Judaism. Abraham lived about 4000 years ago. He believed that there was only one God. In those days, most people believed that there were lots of gods. Abraham went on a long journey because he believed that God was showing him to a new country. (There is more about Abraham on pages 32–3.)

Moses led the Jews when they were escaping from the cruel king of Egypt about 3500 years ago. This is the story which Jews remember at Pesach. (There is more about Moses on pages 34–5.)

Kings

After they had escaped from Egypt, the Jews lived in the desert for many years. At last they made their home in a country called Canaan. This was more or less the area that today we call Israel. It is often called the Promised Land because Jews believe that it is the country which God promised to Abraham.

This map shows the places mentioned in this section and in the next two sections

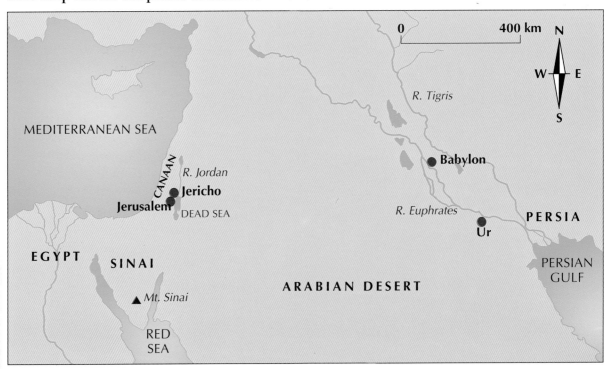

Jews today live in many different countries. This boy comes from Ethiopia

For hundreds of years, they were ruled by kings. Some kings were very good rulers. Others were not. One of the kings was called David. Many Jews still think that David was the best king they have ever had.

Prophets

As well as the kings, there were other men and women who are important in Jewish history. They are the prophets. The prophets told people what God wanted them to do. Sometimes they told people that God wanted them to change the way they lived. All the prophets felt that God was telling them what they had to say.

Enemies

During their history, the Jews' country has been taken over several times. Other nations ruled them. Sometimes Jews were taken away and made to live in their enemies' country. Other Jews left because they did not want to be ruled over by their enemies. They went to find a new life somewhere else. This is one of the reasons why today there are Jews living all over the world.

Test yourself

Who was the first great leader of the Jews?

What did Abraham believe?

Why is the Promised Land called that?

What is a prophet?

Why did some Jews go to live in other countries?

Think it through

1 Why is it not true to talk about one person 'beginning' Judaism? Explain how the religion began.

2 What do you think makes someone a good king? Make a list of reasons why someone might be remembered for being a good ruler.

3 The prophets often told the people about things which were wrong in their country. If you were a prophet in Britain today, what things would you be talking about? Discuss this in groups, then write down your ideas.

Abraham

This section tells you about one of the 'fathers' of Judaism.

Abraham lived about 4000 years ago in a city called Ur. Ur was in the country that today we call Iraq. It was a splendid place with gardens and tall buildings. Abraham was rich, important and respected. He had a very good life, but he was not happy. He saw people in Ur worshipping gods of the sun, the moon and the stars. He felt that the worship included many things which were wrong. For example, human beings were killed because people believed their lives could be an offering to the gods. Abraham became sure that there was another God who was more important. He also became sure that this God did not want to be worshipped in evil ways.

Moon gods in Ur were worshipped in special temples like this, called ziggurats

Abraham's journey

Abraham felt that this God was telling him to leave Ur. He set out on a long journey. He took his wife Sarah, his servants and all his animals. People who wander from place to place are called **nomads**. They do not have a fixed home. In those days, people often lived like this, moving from one place to another to find water for their animals.

Abraham's journey was different. He and his family did not know where they were going, but Abraham believed that God would guide him. Jews believe that God showed Abraham the way to the country called Canaan. This is in the area we now call Israel.

As they travelled, Abraham felt that he was getting to know more about God. He felt that a special relationship was beginning. Jews believe that God promised Abraham

These nomads still live in much the same way as Abraham did

he would become the father of a great nation. All his children and their children for ever would have the same special relationship with God.

New word

Nomads people with no fixed home

Test yourself

Where did Abraham live?

What is a nomad?

Why do people normally live as nomads?

Where did Abraham's journey lead?

What do Jews believe God promised Abraham?

Think it through

1 The city of Ur was very beautiful and Abraham was rich and respected. Explain why he chose to give up his comfortable life to travel to Canaan.

2 Why was Abraham's journey different from those of ordinary nomads? What do you think the people of Ur thought when he set out? What do you think Abraham's wife thought about it?

3 What was the promise God made to Abraham? What does this tell you about why Jews often call him 'Father Abraham'?

Moses

This section tells you about the Jewish leader called Moses.

When Moses was alive, the Jews had been slaves in Egypt for many years. They were treated with great cruelty. The Egyptians were afraid the Jews might try to take over the country. So the king ordered that all Jewish baby boys should be killed as soon as they were born. This was so that they could not grow up to fight against him.

Moses is rescued

When Moses was born, he too should have been killed. But his mother made a plan to save her son. She hid the baby in a basket by the side of the river. The king's daughter came to the river to wash. She found the baby, and took him back to the palace. He lived as if he was the princess's own son.

When Moses grew up, he saw how the Jews were being treated. One day he lost his temper and killed a slave-driver who had beaten a Jew to death. Then he had to leave Egypt, or he would have been killed himself. He stayed away for many years, but at last he became sure that God had work for him to do.

Moses went back to Egypt, and became the Jews' leader. He rescued them and led their escape from Egypt after the ten plagues. This is the story which Jews remember at Pesach. He was their leader when they spent many years as nomads living in the desert. At last, after about 40 years of wandering, they found their way to the country of Canaan, in the area we now call Israel.

The Covenant

Jews believe that when they were in the desert, God gave Moses the Torah. This is the Books of Teaching, and Jews believe it is very important. They believe that the

This Egyptian painting shows the Jews as slaves

The life of Moses

Torah tells them how to live. For Jews, the Torah is part of a special agreement with God called the **Covenant**. It is like a sort of bargain, where both sides make a promise.

Jews believe that God promised he would take special care of the Jews. They would be his 'Chosen People'. This does not mean that they would be his favourites. It means that they were chosen to have extra responsibilities. In return, Jews promised that they would keep the rules of the Torah which God had given them.

Test yourself

Why was Moses saved as a baby?

Why did Moses have to leave Egypt?

What work did God have for Moses?

What did God give Moses in the desert?

What did Jews believe God promised they would be?

Think it through

1 How do you think Moses felt when he had killed the slave-driver?

2 Explain what the Covenant is. Why do Jews believe that it is so important?

3 Moses is remembered as a great Jewish leader. What do you think makes a good leader? Think of as many people as you can who have been good leaders in recent years. Give reasons for your choice.

Persecution

Jews in Nazi Germany wearing the yellow Star of David badge

This section tells you about how Jews have been punished for what they believe.

Persecution means being punished for what you believe. Ever since Judaism began, Jews have been persecuted. No one really knows why. One reason is probably because keeping their religion and their own way of doing things has always been important for Jews. This is the way their religion has survived. Some people may have been frightened of them. Some people have not understood what Jews believe.

Persecution by the Nazis

The worst persecution of the Jews happened when the Nazis were in power in Germany in the 1930s and 1940s. They were led by a man called Adolf Hitler. He believed that people with blond hair and blue eyes were better than everyone else. He began to persecute many other groups. Disliking someone because of their religion or the colour of their skin is called **prejudice**. Hitler was prejudiced against the Jews. He made laws which said Jews were forbidden to do many everyday things.

Jews could not go outside unless they were wearing a yellow Star of David (see page 7). This was so that everyone would know they were Jews. Jews could not own cars. Jews could not ride on buses or trains. Jewish children could not go to school. Jews could not be outside after 9 o'clock at night. The list went on and on.

Then the Nazis decided to get rid of Jews completely. Soldiers went from one house to the next, asking if there were any Jews there. Any Jews they found were taken away. Anyone found hiding Jews was killed. The Jews who were taken away went to special camps. They were not given enough food or clothes, and all their hair was shaved off. Many were killed straight away. Every day, thousands were sent to the gas chambers. Others died from illness or from lack of food.

By the end of World War II, six million Jews had died. One and a half million of them were children. This was one out of every three Jews who had been alive in 1930. Six million is a number too big to imagine, but it is like one in ten of all the people living in Britain today, or every person living in London.

The suffering that Jews have gone through helps to explain why many Jews today are aware of their 'Jewishness'. It also helps to explain why family life is so important to Jews.

This sculpture is part of the memorial at Yad Vashem to Jews killed by the Nazis

'First they came for the Jews
and I did not speak out -
because I was not a Jew.
Then they came for the communists
and I did not speak out -
because I was not a communist.
Then they came for the trade
unionists and I did not speak out -
because I was not a trade unionist.

Then they came for me -
and there was no one left
to speak out for me.'

These words were written by Pastor Neimoller, who was a victim of the Nazis

New words

Persecution being badly treated because of your religion

Prejudice disliking someone because of their religion or the colour of their skin

Test Yourself

What is persecution?

What is prejudice?

Who was the leader of the Nazis?

What did Jews in Germany have to wear?

How many Jews died in World War II?

Think it through

1 Look carefully at the list of things which Jews were forbidden to do. Try to imagine what your life would be like if you could not do these things. What do you think the Nazis were trying to achieve?

2 Look at the quote from Pastor Neimoller on this page. Explain in your own words what the quote means. What do you think Neimoller wanted people to learn?

3 What sort of prejudice can you think of in this country today? Why do you think it happens? How do you feel about it?

Modern Jewish history

This section tells you about recent Jewish history.

Israel

Millions of Jews were killed in World War II. When the war ended, many people thought that Jews should have a country where they could be safe. At that time there was no 'Jewish country' and Jews lived in different countries all over the world. Israel was made a separate country in 1948. The law of Israel says that any Jew in the world has the right to go and live in Israel if he or she wants to.

Making Israel a separate country caused problems·because people were living there already. They are called Arabs. The Arabs thought that the country should still belong to them. Their families had lived there for hundreds of years. Jews feel that the land is theirs, because God promised it to Abraham, and Jews lived there long before the first Arab settled there.

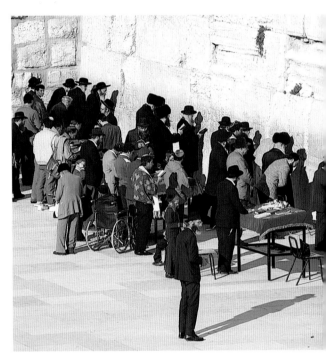

The Western Wall of the Temple is a place of pilgrimage for Jews

The position of Israel

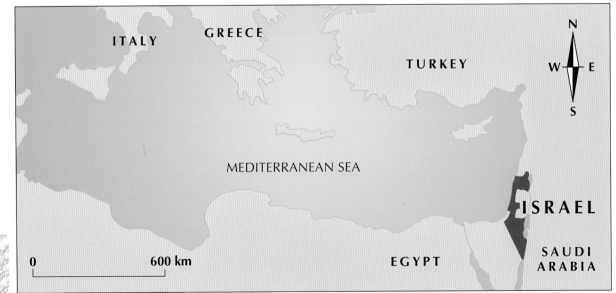

Wars between Jews and Arabs

After Israel became a separate country, there were wars with the countries around it. There have been many attempts to sort out the problems, but none of the agreements have been accepted by all the countries involved. This is why there is still fighting in that part of the world today.

Jerusalem

One reason why there is so much difficulty over the area is that it is very important to three religions. Jews, **Christians** and **Muslims** all believe that important events in their history took place in Jerusalem, the capital city.

In the war of 1967, Jews captured part of Jerusalem, including what remains of the Temple. This was the most important building for Jewish worship. It was destroyed by the Romans in 70 CE. Today only the Western Wall remains. This is an important place of **pilgrimage** for Jews.

This model shows what the Temple in Jerusalem looked like

New words

Christians followers of Jesus
Muslims followers of the religion of Islam
Pilgrimage journey for religious reasons

Test yourself

When was Israel made a separate country?

Who lived there already?

What religion do Muslims follow?

Where was the Temple?

What is a pilgrimage?

Think it through

1 Explain why people felt it was important for Jews to have their own country at the end of World War II. Why do you think the law of Israel says that any Jew can go and live there?

2 Jerusalem is important to Jews, Christians and Muslims. Why do you think this makes it harder to solve the difficulties over the country?

3 What do you think it means to Jews to go to the Western Wall to pray? Think of a place which is important to you. Write a few sentences saying how you feel when you go there.

Judaism today

This section tells you about different Jewish groups in the world today.

Different groups of Jews

In any religion, not all the members share exactly the same beliefs. So different groups of Jews do not all have exactly the same ideas. They all believe in and agree with the most important teachings, but they live their lives in different ways.

Orthodox Jews studying the holy books

The largest group of Jews in the world today are called Orthodox Jews. About three quarters of Jews living in Britain are Orthodox Jews. Other Jews make up smaller groups, for example, Liberal Jews and Reformed Jews. They can be called Progressive Jews.

Orthodox Jews

Orthodox Jews are often called 'strict' Jews. They try to keep all the laws of Judaism as

Inside a Progressive synagogue

40

they have been kept for thousands of years. They believe that the Torah tells people how God wants them to live, and people should follow the rules it gives. For Orthodox Jews, the Torah will never change, although the teaching it gives may be understood in different ways. They believe that through the Torah, people can always know what God wants.

Progressive Jews

Progressive Jews are not all the same, but they all share a belief that Judaism can change. They do not keep all the laws of the Torah as strictly as Orthodox Jews. They believe that if a law does not seem to have a point any longer, it can be changed or forgotten about. The changes usually make it easier to live among people who are not Jews.

In the synagogue

Orthodox and Progressive Jews often live in quite different ways. In the synagogue, they worship in different ways, too. In an Orthodox synagogue, men sit together and women and children sit in another part. In Progressive synagogues, men, women and children sit together. In Progressive synagogues, women sometimes lead the worship, and may become **rabbis**. In Orthodox synagogues, they never do. Orthodox synagogues use more Hebrew in worship.

New word

Rabbis Jewish religious teachers

Test yourself

What is the largest group of Jews called?

What name can be given to the other groups of Jews?

What do Orthodox Jews believe that the Torah shows?

Where do women sit in an Orthodox synagogue?

What is a rabbi?

Think it through

1 Compare the photo opposite with the one of an Orthodox synagogue on page 8. What things can you notice which are the same? What things are different?

2 In Orthodox synagogues, the prayers are said in Hebrew, rather than in the language which the people speak all the time. What advantages and disadvantages can you think of for this?

3 Explain the different ways that Orthodox and Progressive Jews see the Torah. Why might Progressive Jews want to make it easier to live amongst non-Jews? What would Orthodox Jews say to this?

Judaism in the home

This section tells you a little about how Jews follow their religion at home.

Being a Jew is not just about going to the synagogue. It is about the way you live, too. Being Jewish affects every part of a Jew's life. This section looks at two ways in which Jews carry out their beliefs at home.

Mezuzahs

A **mezuzah** is a tiny scroll. It has the prayer called the Shema written on it. The scroll has a cover made of wood, plastic or metal to protect it. The cover with the scroll inside it is fastened next to a door, always on the right hand side.

This man is writing a mezuzah scroll

Some Jews have a mezuzah next to the doors which lead in and out of the house. Other Jews have them fixed to the side of every door in the house, except doors to the bathroom and toilet. As they pass the mezuzah, Jews touch it. This reminds them that God is always there.

Food

The Torah has many laws about food. There are laws about what foods can or cannot be eaten, and how food should be prepared. Many Jews keep these laws very carefully. Jewish shops and more and more supermarkets sell foods which have been made so that they obey Jewish food laws.

Food which Jews are allowed to eat is called **kosher**. All plants are kosher, but not all meat and fish. For meat to be kosher, it must be prepared so that all the blood has been removed from it.

A mezuzah

The foods on the left are kosher, the ones on the right are not

Jews do not eat some meats at all. They do not eat meat and dairy foods (things like butter and milk) at the same time. This means that they would not have butter on a meat sandwich. They usually wait about three hours before 'mixing' them. Plates and dishes are not allowed to mix, either, so many Jews have two sinks or bowls for washing up. They also have two sets of pots and pans, plates and cutlery.

For Jews, preparing food carefully and eating it are ways of worshipping God. They believe God has given the food. For the same reason, they thank him before and after meals.

New words

Kosher food which Jews can eat
Mezuzah tiny scroll of the Shema

Test yourself

What is a mezuzah?

Where is a mezuzah placed?

What does kosher mean?

What is removed from kosher meat?

How long do Jews wait before mixing meat and milk?

Think it through

1 Look carefully at the pictures on page 42. Describe what a mezuzah looks like, and explain why Jews have them near their doors.

2 People once believed that an animal's life was in its blood. Why does this help to explain why blood must be removed from kosher meat? Who do Jews believe the life belongs to?

3 Imagine you are inviting some Jewish friends for a meal. You can buy kosher food. Work in pairs to plan a suitable menu.

Special occasions I

This section tells you about the important services of Bar Mitzvah and Bat Mitzvah.

Names

Jewish babies are always given a special Hebrew name. This name is often chosen to remember someone in the family. They may use the name all the time, or only for important religious occasions, like Bar Mitzvah and Bat Mitzvah.

Bar Mitzvah

A Jewish boy becomes Bar Mitzvah at the age of thirteen. On the Shabbat after his thirteenth birthday, he takes part in the service in the synagogue for the first time. He says the **blessing** before the Torah is read in the service. Like all the prayers in an Orthodox synagogue service, this is in Hebrew. Some boys read passages from the Torah, too. The boy must have practised hard to be able to say the Hebrew words perfectly, especially in front of lots of people! Often, his friends and relatives come to the service, and there may be a special meal afterwards.

A Bar Mitzvah ceremony in a synagogue in Jerusalem

This Bat Mitzvah girl is holding a copy of the holy books which she has decorated

Bar Mitzvah means 'Son of the Commandments'. Once he has reached this age, a Jewish boy is expected to obey all the Jewish laws. He is counted as a man, and can be one of the ten men who must be present before a full service can be held in Orthodox synagogues.

Bat Mitzvah

A Jewish girl becomes Bat Mitzvah at the age of twelve. Bat Mitzvah means 'Daughter of the Commandments'. Not all Orthodox synagogues have a special service for girls. If there is one, it will be held on a Sunday, rather than Shabbat, which is a Saturday. Girls do not read from the Torah in an Orthodox synagogue. In Progressive synagogues, there is no difference between the services held for boys and girls. A party for friends and relations is usually held afterwards.

New word

Blessing special prayer

Test yourself

What does Bar Mitzvah mean?

What does Bat Mitzvah mean?

What does a boy do at his Bar Mitzvah?

What is a blessing?

Think it through

1 What do you think it means to be a Son or Daughter of the Commandments?

2 A Jewish boy is counted as an adult when he is thirteen. What do you think about this? How old do you think someone should be before they are thought to be an adult?

3 Why do you think Jews have special Hebrew names as well as their everyday names? Do you know what your name means? Was there a special reason why you were given the name you have?

Special occasions II

This section tells you about what happens at special events in a Jew's life.

Marriage

A Jewish wedding usually takes place in a synagogue. It is led by a rabbi. The couple who are getting married stand under a special covering called a **huppah**. It is beautifully decorated, and is a symbol of the home they will share.

The couple drink from a glass of wine which has had a blessing said over it. Then the marriage promises are read out, in which the bridegroom promises to look after his wife. The bride and groom sign them. The bridegroom gives the bride a ring which she wears on the first finger of her right hand.

At the end of the service, the bridegroom steps on a wine glass and breaks it. (It is wrapped in a cloth for safety.) No one really knows why this happens, but it has been part of the marriage service for hundreds of years. It reminds the couple

The bride and groom stand under the huppah

Jewish graves

that there will be difficult things as well as good things in their life and that they must face them together.

Divorce

If a couple are having problems, friends and relations do their best to help them save their marriage. If divorce cannot be avoided, the husband gives the wife a certificate of divorce. This is the only way that a Jewish marriage can be ended. A Jew who has been divorced is allowed to remarry.

Death

Jews believe that a funeral service should be held as soon as possible after someone dies. If possible, it should be within 24 hours. Services are simple, because Jews believe there should be no difference between rich and poor. Everyone has to die.

Most Jews do not agree with **cremation** (burning a dead body) because they think it destroys what God has made. Although Jews believe in life after death, teaching about it is not a very important part of the religion. They think it is better to think about how you live now, rather than worry about what happens afterwards.

Test yourself

What is a huppah?

Where does a Jewish woman wear her wedding ring?

What does breaking the glass mean?

When do Jewish funerals take place?

What is cremation?

Think it through

1 Use the picture on the opposite page to help you describe what a huppah looks like. Explain why a couple who are getting married stand under a huppah.

2 Design a card which you could send to a Jewish couple for their wedding. Try to find out the Hebrew greeting which Jews would use.

3 What do Jews believe about life after death? What do you believe about it? Why?

Glossary

The page numbers tell you where you can find out most about the words.

Adonai 'Lord' – Jewish name for God   page 6

Adultery sexual relationship outside marriage   page 29

Ark cupboard where the scrolls are kept   page 8

Atonement making up for something you have done wrong   page 16

Bimah raised part of the floor where the reading desk is   page 8

Blessing special power   page 44

Challah bread special bread for Shabbat   page 14

Christians followers of Jesus   page 39

Commandments important rules   page 28

Covenant special agreement made between God and the Jews   page 35

Cremation burning a body after death   page 47

Dreidle four-sided spinning top   page 21

Eternal lasting for ever   page 6

Fast go without food and drink for religious reasons   page 17

Greggors rattles used by children at Purim   page 23

Hanukiah candlestick with eight branches used at Hanukkah   page 20

Havdalah prayer said at the end of Shabbat   page 15

Hebrew language of the Jews   page 8

Holy to do with God   page 8

Huppah covering used for marriage service   page 46

Idols false gods (often statues)   page 28

Kiddush prayer which begins the Shabbat meal   page 14

Kippah skull cap   page 11

Kosher food which Jews can eat   page 42

Leaven yeast or baking powder which makes dough rise   page 26

Lulav collection of branches for Sukkot   page 19

Matzot 'crackers' of bread made without leaven (one is a matzah)   page 26

Menorah candlestick with seven branches   page 7

Mezuzah tiny scroll of the Shema   page 42

Miracle event which can't be explained but which shows God's power   page 20

Muslims followers of the religion of Islam   page 39

Nomads people with no fixed home   page 32

Parchment writing surface made from animal skin   page 8

Persecution being badly treated because of your religion   page 36

Pilgrimage journey for religious reasons   page 39

Plague disasters believed to be sent by God   page 24

Prejudice disliking someone because of their religion or the colour of their skin   page 36

Prophets people who tell others how God wants them to live   page 13

Psalms sorts of poems used in worship   page 10

Rabbis Jewish religious teachers   page 41

Scrolls rolled up 'books' on which the Torah is written   page 8

Seder special Pesach meal   page 26

Shema most important Jewish prayer   page 7

Shofar instrument made from a ram's horn   page 16

Sukkah sort of hut (plural sukkot)   page 18

Synagogue Jewish place of worship   page 8

Symbol something that stands for something else   page 7

Tallit prayer robe   page 11

Tefillin small leather boxes which contain writings from the Torah (one is called a tefillah)   page 11

Temple most important place of worship for Jews   page 7

Tenakh name for the Jewish holy books   page 12

Torah Books of Teaching (part of the Jewish holy books)   page 8

Writings third part of the Jewish holy books   page 13